SPEAK LIKE THE GREATS

SHORT STORIES TO INSPIRE YOU, AND IN TURN, OTHERS

KEVIN ABDULRAHMAN

**PUBLIC SPEAKING COACH TO CEOS,
WORLD LEADERS, PRESIDENTS & ROYALTY**

Copyright © 2018 Kevin Abdulrahman
All rights reserved.

KEVIN ABDULRAHMAN

MORE BOOKS BY KEVIN ABDULRAHMAN

60 Minutes To Better Public Speaking

Public Speaking Tips

Leadership: A Beginner's Guide To Becoming A Great Leader

Get Inspired, Get Informed & Get Going!!!

Think. Do. Be. Different

No One Dies A Virgin

What Ever You're Into

Winning The Game Of Life

THE ROLE OF THE STORYTELLER IS TO **AWAKEN** THE STORYTELLER IN OTHERS

Jack Zipes

KEVIN ABDULRAHMAN

DEDICATION

As a leader, you're expected to communicate with impact.

The mark of great leaders has always been their ability to share stories.

This book is for every leader, who aspires to make a mark.

To become, one of *The Greats*.

SPEAK LIKE THE GREATS

PREFACE

This is how the book came about.

Reason Number 1

As a motivational speaker, I deliver hundreds of keynote speeches to forward thinking companies and leading governments, all over the world.

On one such event, I was seated in the audience listening to the C-Suite executives of a company, deliver their talks.

These executives weren't representing a mom-and-pop shop.

This was an international, household brand - A 'Fortune 50' company.

You guessed it.

One after another, they got on stage.

And they put the audience to sleep - the lucky ones.

The unlucky folks, had to endure a combination of boredom and having all their senses assaulted.

It was clear that none of these executives had actually received proper Leadership Communication training.

Nor did they think they needed it.

It was evident in their misguided over-confidence.

The last of the executives stepped up on stage.

He began by saying, "I'm going to share an inspirational story".

I thought to myself, "Finally, this guy is going to breathe some life into the event".

My excitement was short lived.

A few slides in, it became apparent that although he had the right idea, it was only just that - An idea.

He was unable to string two sentences together.

He told his 'story'.

It was supposed to be inspirational.

Instead, it was butchered.

The audience were totally lost.

The story, fell flat on its face.

Just as the audience's faces did, into their phones.

The inspiration?- Well, it never even made it through the doors.

This 'leader' lacked the skill to craft and tell a great story.

The story of John Stephen Akhwari.

If his intended story was designed to (and it could have) help leaders move mountains, all this executive managed to do, was move the audience into a coma.

A common fate I've witnessed. Even with leaders that attempt to tell a story.

So I got thinking…

Reason Number 2

As a public speaking coach and advisor to CEOs, world leaders, presidents and royalty, I establish with them, the power of storytelling.

We deliberate on how we should incorporate it into their speeches and presentations.

I work with them on crafting stories that are personal, and powerful.

On a number of occasions, after having brainstormed some ideas, I found myself looking up, only to see a deep wave of concern flooding their eyes.

Followed by them nervously saying, "But Kev, it's easy for you to tell stories. You've been doing it for 20+ years".

SPEAK LIKE THE GREATS

It is much easier for me, because I've been speaking, coaching and crafting speeches for some time now.

I recognized this reality.

I also recognized, their reality.

I recognized their concerns.

I also understood how critical storytelling is for their speeches.

So to get the ball rolling, I started sharing some stories to help them out.

Stories that I had read.

Stories that I had heard.

Stories that I had seen being told.

Stories that had helped me speak to impact, inform, influence and inspire tens of thousands of people at any given event.

Stories that I had used to help teams come together, to go from good to great.

Stories that moved people's hearts and minds.

So I got thinking…

These two reasons led to the creation of a practical book.

Not a book that tells you the importance of storytelling (you should know this already).

But a book that has a compilation of stories.

Short stories.

Simple and easy to follow stories.

Stories that will touch the hearts and minds of anyone. Including yours.

Stories that could then help you, deliver your message.

And make it, forever memorable.

As a leader, you can pick and weave any of following stories into your speech.

To deliver your message with impact.

Read it. Practice it. Deliver it.

Sure, the best stories are the stories that you've lived through.

But these stories will form the stepping stones for you to practice.

To first, tell the stories in the way it's currently structured.

Then with plenty of practice, delivering the stories in your own way.

And overtime, delivering powerful stories that are personal to you.

And yes, I've included the inspirational story of John Stephen Akhwari.

I hope that his story, amongst all the others, inspire you.

And I hope that you will be able to then tell these stories in a way that will help you ignite your audience to action.

To help you move mountains.

SPEAK LIKE THE GREATS
A SIMPLE GUIDE

The stories you'll read will loosely fall under one, or many of the following categories:

Acceptance	Action	Attitude	Ambition
Appreciation	Belief	Challenges	Care
Change	Communication	Compassion	Courage
Creativity	Culture	Customer service	Discipline
Dreams	Empowerment	Empathy	Entrepreneurship
Excellence	Failure	Family	Gratitude
Giving	Happiness	Inspiration	Integrity
Leadership	Legacy	Life	Love
Mastery	Mindset	Persistence	Perspective
Persuasion	Purpose	Relationships	Self-confidence
Stress	Success	Teamwork	Vision

And dozens of others. You're smart. You'll figure it out.

The stories are simple. By design.

Depending on the key message you are delivering, choose a story that best fits.

It should feel natural.

It should make sense.

It should need, no explaining.

Deliver the story. And then, you can drive home the message you wish to make.

At the end of each story, I've included a <u>sample</u> 'Take Home Message' to help get your creative juices flowing.

Every story has more than one lesson or angle to it.

You can edit, change or say it as it is. Your call.

I hope the stories inspire you.

And in turn, help you speak to impact, inform, influence and inspire your audience.

Enjo

KEVIN ABDULRAHMAN

EVERY STORY YOU TELL

IS YOUR OWN STORY

Joseph Campbell

SPEAK LIKE THE GREATS
THE POWER OF STORYTELLING

Rob Walker and Joshua Glenn wanted to find out:

Could storytelling add desirability?

Could it add value?

Could it add significance?

They bought 200 objects from thrift stores and garage sales.

The average price of each, around $1.

Then, they asked two hundred creative writers to write a fictional story for each object.

All 200 objects were listed on eBay. Each with it's accompanying story.

The results?

One object, a globe paperweight, was purchased for $1.49. It sold for $197.50.

The only addition. The only difference. Was it's accompanying story.

Was it a fluke? Maybe this was a 'wanted' object? What about the other objects?

The 200 objects were purchased for a total of $129.

They sold for over $8,000.

That's over 6000% - The only difference? Each object had a story.

Take Home Message:

Storytelling increases desirability

Storytelling increases value.

Storytelling adds significance.

Storytelling has significance.

The next time you plan to communicate in the boardroom, present to your peers or stand up to speak in front of an audience, ask yourself - "What story can I tell to add significance to my message?"

KEVIN ABDULRAHMAN
WHAT KIND OF A PERSON DO YOU WANT TO BE?

A young lady was going through tough times.

She decided to visit her Grandma for some care, comfort and love.

She began to tell her Grandma about all the obstacles she was facing.

How one obstacle followed the other.

How it seemed never ending.

How drained she was feeling.

Hearing this, and without saying a word, the Grandma rose and went to the kitchen.

She placed three small pots of water on the stove.

Into the first pot went a carrot. The second, an egg. The third, some coffee beans.

Twenty minutes later the Grandma took out the carrot, egg, and poured a small cup of coffee.

"What do you see?", said the Grandma.

"A carrot, an egg and some coffee", said the granddaughter.

"Feel the carrot, peel the egg and try the coffee", said the Grandma.

The young lady felt the carrot. What was once hard, had become soft.

The egg's surface looked the same. But the soft inside had become hard.

And the coffee? Well it had spread its flavor and aroma into the water.

That's when the Grandma said, "The same hot water that softens the carrot, hardens the egg. The same hot water that hardens the egg, makes the coffee spread".

SPEAK LIKE THE GREATS

Take Home Message:

You have zero control about the obstacles, challenges, hardships and heartbreaks - the hot water in your life.

But you have all the control, when it comes to choosing the kind of person you want to be.

You can choose to go soft and weak like the carrot.

You can choose to harden up, become guarded and cold, like the egg.

Or you can choose to change your environment, like the coffee beans.

What kind of a person will you choose to be?

KEVIN ABDULRAHMAN
STOP IT ALREADY

For as long he could remember, a wise man had people come up to him and complain about the problems in their lives.

Over time, he noticed a pattern.

These people, whoever they were, would complain about the same set of problems.

Over, and over, and over again.

So, one day, he decided to tell them a joke, to cheer them up - lighten the mood a little bit.

It worked.

Every person that heard the joke, roared in laughter.

Next time they visited, the wise man would tell them the same joke.

With time, the laughters gradually turned down in notches.

Then, it was no longer a laugh but traces of smiles with "yeah, yeah, we know it already".

There came a time where no one laughed.

At which point, the wise man smiled.

That's when he said, "You can't laugh at the same joke over and over again.

Why are you then, always complaining about the same set of problems?"

SPEAK LIKE THE GREATS

Take Home Message:

You can continue to complain about what you lack.

You can continue to complain about how things are stacked against you.

You can continue to complain how it's all unfair.

You can continue to complain, for the sake of complaining.

Or.

You can start looking for different opportunities.

You can start making different connections.

You can start having different conversations.

You can start implementing different approaches.

Complaining alone, changes nothing.

If nothing changes, then nothing changes.

KEVIN ABDULRAHMAN
BAD NEWS, GOOD NEWS, LET'S SEE

For years, a farmer used his horse to help with the daily work on the farm.

One day the farmer's horse took off.

On hearing the news, the neighbor came by to check up on the farmer.

"I heard about the bad news", he said.

"Bad news? Good News? Let's see", replied the farmer.

The neighbor thought it was a rather strange answer.

Within a few days, the farmer's horse returned, bringing along with it a group of wild horses.

"Ahh, good news. Look at your new found fortune", the neighbor was quick to remark.

"Bad news? Good News? Let's see", replied the farmer.

The following day, the farmer's eldest son decided to get on one of the wild horses.

No sooner than getting on, was he thrown off, ending up with a broken leg.

The neighbor came by to sympathize with the farmer's terrible turn of events.

"I heard the bad news about your son's broken leg", sympathized the neighbor.

"Bad news? Good News? Let's see", were the farmer's only words.

A few days later the military passed through the village drafting young capable men into the army.

The farmer's eldest son was passed upon.

He was deemed unfit, because of his broken leg.

The neighbor couldn't believe the farmers good luck. Surely now, the farmer must have been ecstatic?

In asking the farmer, his response remained, "Bad news? Good News? Let's see".

SPEAK LIKE THE GREATS

Take Home Message:

Far too often we get attached to the outcome of our days.

Some are good. Some aren't.

Sometimes, we over celebrate.

Sometimes, we spend far too long moping around.

You might not like or be happy with the turn of events.

You might not get what you expect or hope for.

Learn to remain unattached to any given outcome. Good or bad.

With every turn, no matter how bleak, comes an opportunity.

Bad News?

Good News?

Let's see.

KEVIN ABDULRAHMAN
LET'S NOT FORGET THOSE THAT MATTER

Late from work, a busy executive arrived home.

As usual, he never made it to family dinners.

His four-year-old daughter would also be asleep by then.

She rarely saw him.

One evening, she was awake.

As the father arrived home, she ran out to greet, and hug him.

"Daddy, how much do you earn an hour?", she asked.

"$30 an hour", the father replied.

"But I never get to see you Daddy", said the daughter.

"I know baby. But I'm doing all of this for you, my little angel", replied the father.

And so…. Nothing changed.

The man continued coming home late from work every night.

One evening, the daughter was awake again.

She ran to her father and gave him a big hug.

She then went to her room, and ran back.

This time she came to her father with her 'teeny weeny fists' full of coins.

Surprised, the father asked, "What do you have here angel?"

Her reply,

"I have been saving for a long time Daddy.

I now have $30.

Will you now spend an hour with me?"

SPEAK LIKE THE GREATS

Take Home Message:

"Lost time", said Benjamin Franklin, "is never found again".

In our quest to achieve, succeed and be recognized.

Let's always remember our real reasons.

Why we do what we do.

The people whom we do it for.

The people that matter to us the most.

Let's not forget how important they are in our lives.

And that the best thing we could ever do for those who matter, isn't to give them things.

But to give them, ourselves.

To give them, our time.

KEVIN ABDULRAHMAN
GET UP OR SHUT UP

Every day, a young man walked past his neighbor's home.

Every day, he would hear the neighbor's dog howling from the porch.

One day the young man decided to visit his neighbor.

The neighbor was an older fellow.

There he was peacefully having his coffee on the porch.

The young man asked, "Why is your dog howling every day? He must be in pain".

The older fellow took a sip from his cup, smiled and said,

"Yes, I'm aware of it. The dog is sitting on a nail".

The younger man quizzed, "Well, why doesn't he get up and get off the nail then?"

With another sip the older fellow replied, "Because it's hurting him, but not enough, for him to move".

Take Home Message:

What nails are you sitting on in your life?

What are you complaining and doing nothing about?

How much longer will you continue to sit on the nails in your life?

If it really hurts, get up.

Move.

YOUR AIM MUST BE TO MOVE PEOPLE, NOT YOUR PRODUCT OR PROPERTY

KEVIN ABDULRAHMAN
A MEMORABLE MOMENT

Like many smart companies, Starbucks is conscious about the importance of customer experience. How small touches and connections make all the difference.

This is one of the reasons why when you go in to one of their stores and order your coffee, the barista writes your name down on the cup. To create a connection - and yes, even when they get it wrong.

One day a regular customer stopped by his local Starbucks.
The barista noticed him coming in.
She had served him, once before.
Quickly she started writing something down on a piece of paper.

The customer wondered for a moment, as he watched the barista scribble down a note.

"Maybe the barista had a question for me", he thought.

When the barista handed him the note, the customer was shocked.
The note read, "I've been learning ASL (American Sign Language) just so you can have the same experience as everyone else".

This customer was deaf.
But having served him once before, the barista had gone home, and spent over three hours of her own time, learning the basics of sign language.

Just for one customer.
Just, for one order.

To the customer, the barista's gesture meant everything.
It was so touching and memorable.

SPEAK LIKE THE GREATS

So much so, that the customer saved, and even, framed her note.

The barista didn't think much of what she did.
In her mind, he was her customer.
And like every other customer, he deserved to have the same experience and connection.

The very least she could do, she thought, was learn to ask him what he wants to drink.

Now, he could, just like anyone else, place his order and feel the connection and experience that everyone else feels when they go to Starbucks.

Take Home Message:
Going that extra mile doesn't mean moving mountains, to make an impression.
But it could feel like it for the person on the receiving end.
Going the extra mile isn't something that can be told, trained or forced upon you.
But it is something, you can choose to do.
Going the extra mile doesn't mean that it should be done for rewards and recognition.
But it is something you can do for the satisfaction you get, from the act itself.

KEVIN ABDULRAHMAN
AN UTTER FAILURE

At 21, he fails in business.

At 22, he loses a legislative race.

At 24, he fails in business again.

At 26, he has to handle the passing away of his sweetheart.

At 27, he has a nervous breakdown.

At 34, he loses a congressional race.

At 45, he loses a senatorial race.

At 47, he goes for the role of Vice President and fails.

And right about now, you're thinking, this guy, who ever he is, should really take a seat and have a break.

But no.

Instead, at 49, he goes for and loses, another senatorial race.

But... At 52, he becomes the President of the United States of America.

You know this utter failure, as the man who has since inspired his future presidents.

You know him as Abraham Lincoln.

Take Home Message:

In life, as in business, you will be handed defeat after defeat.

You can let it get to you.

You can stop trying.

Or you can do what Lincoln did. Get up, and try again.

Next time you are facing a crushing defeat, think, what would Lincoln do?

Because to Lincoln, defeat was only ever a detour, not a dead-end.

PURPOSEFUL STORYTELLING ISN'T SHOW BUSINESS, IT'S GOOD BUSINESS

Peter Guber

KEVIN ABDULRAHMAN
WANTING THE BEST

A group of MBA students were deep in discussion before class.

Walking in, the professor overheard his students talking about different aspects of their lives.

Many of them were complaining about their jobs, assignments and families.

Noticing that these students were so focussed on comparing problems, he said, "It seems like we could all benefit from starting the class with a cup of coffee".

They all agreed.

Pots of coffee were brought out. And a large range of cups were made available.

Far more than what was needed. Glass cups. Porcelain cups, plastic cups.

The teacher told the students to help themselves.

Once everyone had their cups of coffee, he pointed out.

"Isn't it interesting that all the 'nice looking' cups have been taken, and what's left are the plain or 'cheap looking' ones.

And it's ok, you all want the best for yourselves.

Just remember that this could very well be the source of your complaining.

Coffee is what you all wanted.

Yet, none of the cups here add any value or taste to the coffee.

You wanted coffee. Not the cups. Yet subconsciously, getting a great cup became important.

The things I heard you complaining about. Your jobs, assignments, challenges with families. They are all the cups.

You are so focussed on the cup, when what really matters is the coffee".

SPEAK LIKE THE GREATS

Take Home Message:

Never lose sight of what really is of importance. To you.

You will never find happiness concentrating on the cup.

What you do not have.

What it could have been.

What it should have been.

What others have compare to you.

What matters isn't having the best.

It's the choice of making the best, with what you have.

Concentrate on the coffee, and making the most out of it.

What ever cup you may end drinking from, remember to enjoy the coffee.

KEVIN ABDULRAHMAN
THE POWER TO PERSUADE

One day, the wind approached the sun with a challenge.

The wind claimed his great strength. That he could achieve anything with his power.

The sun   she believed in the power of being gentle.

The wind? He wanted to prove a point.

"Look, you see that man wearing a jacket.

Who ever can make the man take off his jacket, wins"

The wind continued.

"I can use my strength, and with ease, remove his jacket. Watch me".

And so the wind began, flexing all his muscles.

He started blowing hard. The wind was really strong.

The man had to work hard not to fall on his back.

The wind worked harder. But the man kept holding on tight.

The harder the wind blew, the harder the man held on to his jacket.

After some time, the wind got tired and gave up in despair.

The man? He still held 'firmly' onto his jacket.

The sun then took a more gentle approach.

From behind the clouds, she started to beam.

Gently. She began to shine. Getting brighter and hotter.

After some time, the man voluntarily took off his jacket and sought some shade to rest in.

Take Home Message

Remember, a man against his own will, is of the same opinion still.

You can try forcing people with your thoughts and opinions.

As a person in position, it maybe easy for you to command and demand.

But real leaders, those who are able to get their people's buy in,

Those who are able to have their entire work-force behind them,

SPEAK LIKE THE GREATS

They understand that there are many ways to persuade people.

And very often, the most powerful approach, is when you use the least power.
It's when you use the power of being gentle.

Next time, you want to persuade others to your way of thinking, ask yourself-
Are you being the wind?
Or are you being the sun?

KEVIN ABDULRAHMAN
SEEKING CHANGE

A traveler left his city and arrived at the outskirts of a new city.

On his arrival, he saw an old man and asked him, "Old man, tell me about the people of this city?"

The old man replied by asking, "Young traveler, tell me about the people of the city you've come from?"

The traveler said, "The people were miserable, terrible, negative, dishonest and unhelpful. I am glad to have left that city".

The old man sheepishly replied, "Then I'm afraid to say that the people of this city will be no different".

A few days went by, and another traveler passed by asking the old man the same question, "Old man, tell me about the people of this city?"

The old man replied by asking, "Young traveler, tell me about the people of the city you've come from?"

This traveler said, "The people were amazing. Such positive people, giving, helpful and honest. I am so sad to have left that city".

The old man replied with a smile, "Fear not young traveler, for the people of this city will be just the same".

Take Home Message:

Whether you are moving from country to country, city to city, suburb to suburb, company to company or from one team to another - You take you with you.

If change is what you really seek, start from within.

SPEAK LIKE THE GREATS
DON'T BE QUICK TO JUDGE

A nine-year-old boy walks into a coffeeshop.

It's a busy time with many of the tables needing service.

The waitress directs the boy to a free table.

She offers him the menu and says that she will be back in a few minutes.

The boy studies the menu.

When the waitress arrives, he asks, "Excuse me Miss, how much is a caramel sundae?"

"Well, that's four dollars and fifty cents", says the waitress.

"Hmmm", says the boy, as he takes his hand out of his pocket to count all his coins.

Impatiently, the waitress waits for the young boy.

He looks up at her, and asks, "What about just a plain ice cream Miss?"

"Four dollars", she snaps back at him.

He looks down to re-count his coins again, and confirms how much he has.

He looks up at her and says, "OK. I guess I will just have a plain ice cream then".

The waitress goes and brings the ice cream along with the bill, which she places on the table.

The young boy eats his ice cream, puts all his coins on the table and leaves.

When the waitress comes back to clear the table, her eyes begin to well up.

Neatly placed next to the bill, are the boy's coins.

Everything he had.

Not four dollars.

But four dollars and fifty cents.

Her tip included.

Take Home Message:

In life, we will find ourselves quick to judge others.

We don't know people.

We don't know their past.

We don't know their experiences.

We don't know, what they are going through.

Perhaps if we did, we would change our behavior, attitude and judgement towards them.

The next time you find yourself judging someone, stop.

Instead, take a moment, and get to know them.

You might change your attitude towards them.

And walk away with a completely different picture.

SPEAK LIKE THE GREATS
YOUNGEST BILLIONAIRE

He became the youngest billionaire of his time.
When asked to share the secret to his success, the man replied:

There is no secret to success.
I worked hard on an idea to get it as good as I could.
Then, I knocked on door after door.
I ended up showing my idea to 1200 people.
900 said no.
300 showed some interest.
Only 85 people actually did anything, by looking deeper into it.
Of those, only 30 took it to a serious stage.
11 of them, made me a multimillionaire.

The you billionaire in question?
Bill Gates.

Take Home Message:
Bill Gates is no different than anyone else.
He worked hard to have something good.
He knocked on door after door. Literally.
He heard more 'No's' than you.
But he didn't accept it.
Neither should you.

The reality is simple.
Some will. Some won't. Who cares.
Keep knocking.
With every no, you get closer to a yes.

KEVIN ABDULRAHMAN
WHAT CAN WE LEARN FROM THE GEESE

When it's migration season, you'll notice flocks of geese flying in a V-formation.
Science has found that they do it for good reason.

In their teams, with every flap, each bird creates an uplift for the one behind it.
They fly on the thrust from one another.
In this formation the geese are able to cover over 70 percent more distance compared to if they were flying alone.

For encouragement, the geese at the back honk, so that the ones in the front keep up their pace.

When the leading goose gets tired, it takes a break and rotates with another goose for it to take the lead. They keep taking turns to keep their pace and avoid fatigue.

When a goose gets wounded or ill, it doesn't fall out of formation alone.
Oh no.
It's always accompanied by others who will care for it until it either gets better or passes away.
Only then, would they continue up to join their formation or the next team.

SPEAK LIKE THE GREATS

Take Home Message:

As humans, we could benefit from the example and reminder these geese set.

To lead. Ourselves, and others.

To encourage one another.

To be there for each other.

To never leave anyone behind.

All for one. One for all.

Every one of you can contribute to the vision and flight of your team.

You can move faster, and farther, together, as a team.

Just think, how much more powerful you can become as a team, if you followed the lead of the migrating geese?

THE PURPOSE OF A STORYTELLER IS NOT TO TELL YOU HOW TO THINK, BUT TO GIVE YOU QUESTIONS TO THINK UPON

Brandon Sanderson

SPEAK LIKE THE GREATS
A CHEQUE FOR HALF A MILLION

In a lot of debt, a businessman goes to the park for some time out.

He finds a bench to sit on, as thoughts of creditors, suppliers, partners and customers all come flooding in.

Troubled, with head in hands, low in confidence, he wonders whether bankruptcy is imminent?

Then, he hears a voice that says, "It appears that you're going through some tough times".

As the businessman looks up, he notices an old man sitting next to him.

The businessman pours his heart out. Sharing the range of pressures he's facing.

Without uttering a word, the old man takes out his cheque book, and begins writing.

He tears out a cheque, and hands it over to the businessman.

HALF A MILLION DOLLARS

"Take the money. Consider it a loan for one year. Meet me here one year from now, and pay it back". The old man gets up, turns away and disappears.

Looking back down at the cheque, the businessman notices the name and signature: John D. Rockefeller.

One of the richest men in the world.

"Boom. Cashing this cheque will make all my problems go away", the businessman thinks.

And then he deliberates.

"You know what, I'm not going to use this cheque, just yet. It will always be there if I really need it. Instead, I'm going to see how I can make things work with the confidence of knowing, that if I ever really need the money, I can just cash the cheque.

With a renewed positive outlook and revived confidence, the businessman begins working in a different light.

Negotiations, decisions, deal making, partnerships, communication.

All coming from a place of strength.

All coming, from a place of assurance and confidence.

In the back of his mind, there is a half-a-million dollar cheque that can be cashed, at any moment.

Within a few months, the businessman is back on track.

Out of debt.

And making money.

A year passes and so the businessman heads to the park.

Enthusiastic to meet the old man. To thank him for being so generous.

More importantly, he is proud to tell him that he never had to cash his cheque.

The businessman arrives to the park and waits. Cheque in hand.

And there he is, the old man, walking towards the businessman.

Only this time, the old man isn't alone.

A nurse is hastily running, trying to catch up to him.

As they all meet, the nurse tells the businessman, "I'm glad I got him. I hope he hasn't been bothering you. Every so often, the old man wanders off from the mental hospital and comes to the park. When he finds an ear that would listen, he tells them that he is John D. Rockefeller".

The businessman stands still in his tracks.
He's in shock.
He soon realizes that the cheque, unreal as it was, had turned his mindset, confidence and business around.

His thoughts, decisions and actions were based on the belief that he had a half-million-dollar war chest that he could use when ever he needed it.
He felt that power, the entire year - All from an unreal check.

Take Home Message:
Real or not, the businessman's life was turned around because of the belief, thought process, confidence to decide and power to take action, as if, he had half-a-million dollars behind him.

Such is the power that is your mind.
The power to make moves from a place of strength.
The power to be self-confident.

Instead of being down and frustrated about the position you're in today, change your outlook.
Ask yourself, "How would you operate, if you had a cheque for half-a-million dollars?
How would you go about your days if you had all that you needed?
What thoughts would you have?
What decisions would you make?
What actions would you take?"

Go on and do just that.

KEVIN ABDULRAHMAN
REMEMBER YOUR ROCKS

Students started filling up the classroom.
When it was time, the teacher walked to the front of the class to begin.

In front of him was an empty jar.
Without saying a word, he picked up some rocks and placed them in the jar.
When the jar was full, he looked up and asked the students, "Is the jar full?"

Going by what they were all seeing. Indeed the jar was full.
In unison they all nodded.

The teacher then proceeded to empty a bag of small pebbles into the jar filling up the spaces between the rocks.
When all the pebbles were added in the jar, the teacher asked again, "Is the jar full?"

This time, the students thought, it's definitely full.
They all confirmed, "Yes it's full".

The teacher then reached out for a bag of sand and emptied the sand into the jar.
The sand got into all the tiny spaces between the rocks and the pebbles.
Now the teachers asked, "Is it full?"

The students were certain, "It's full"

The teacher then said.
"The rocks represent the important things in your life. Your health. Family. Friends. Time with your loved ones. Pursuing your passion. Things that are of significance.

SPEAK LIKE THE GREATS

The pebbles represent the other important things that are secondary, like your jobs, your home, your car, your responsibilities.

And the sand, well, that's all the little things in your day to day life that consume your time, focus and energy. The sand represents, insignificance. All the small stuff that takes up a lot of space.

If you fill the jar with sand, there will be no space for your rocks and pebbles.

If you focus on the insignificant things, you leave no space for what matters, the significant things.

The important things. The things that matter.

Take Home Message:
Recognize your priorities.
Fill your life with what's important first.
If you don't, sand will fill up your jar every day, leaving very little space for your rocks and pebbles.

Spend time with your loved ones.
Talk to your children.
Go to dinner with your partner.
Take care of yourself.
Invest in relationships.

Make sure you fill your jar with what's significant.
With what matters the most first.
The rocks in your life.

X

A busy factory line came to a screeching halt.

Something was wrong.

An expert was located and contacted to immediately provide her assistance.

After a brief inspection, she calls in the line managers, sketches on the board and marks the point of problem.

This is your faulty point.

Change it and everything will move smoothly like before.

Immediately the point was located and fixed.

Everything was back to normal.

In and out in 30 minutes.

The next day the experts' bill was received.

To the shock of Management it read : TEN THOUSAND DOLLARS.

The manager called the expert and said,

"You were only here for 30 minutes. You took a walk around. And then sketched on our board and marked a 'X' as the point of the problem.

We don't understand how you arrived at this figure.

Can you send us an itemized version of the bill?"

The next hour a new bill was received.

It read:

ONE DOLLAR - for marking the X

NINE THOUSAND NINE HUNDRED AND NINETY NINE DOLLARS - for knowing where to put the X.

SPEAK LIKE THE GREATS

Take Home Message:

Understand that there is a difference between price and value.

You may consider making this investment as expensive.

In your mind, you might be comparing this investment with other 'cheaper' quotes you have received.

But let me ask you, which would you prefer?

Someone who will spend endless hours trying to figure out the problem.

Look and act busy.

And after all the time wasted, lack the experience to actually deliver results.

And if they do, they end up costing you more, in time and lost opportunities.

OR

Would you prefer making an investment in knowing that you are dealing with a professional.

Someone who has fought this battle before.

Someone who knows what to look for.

Someone who knows where to mark the X, turn things around and get you guaranteed results in the shortest possible time?

Just remember, the cheapest option may end costing you the most.

Focus on value. Not price.

Focus, on results.

KEVIN ABDULRAHMAN
NAILS IN THE FENCE

A son with a temper.
A father with a thought.

The father handed his son a bag of nails and said, "Son, every time you get angry, I want you to hammer a nail into the fence".
At the end of the first day. The son had hammered in 40 nails.
Over the coming days, and then weeks, the son came to a realization.
Learning to control his anger was far less effort, than having to hammer in a nail, every time he lost his temper.

And so with every day, less and less nails were hammered in.
The day arrived, when the son didn't get angry. For the whole day.

Proud, he rushed to his father to tell him of the good news.

The father told his son, "I want you to now, start removing a nail for everyday that you don't lose your temper".

And so as the weeks and months went by, the son was able to remove all the nails.
The day arrived when he told his father that all the nails were gone.

"Well done Son", said the father as he walked over with him to the fence.
"I'm proud of you.
But take a look of what remains.
Look at the holes that remain on the fence.
Just remember that when we get angry with others, we say things that very often, we don't mean.
But still, it leaves a hole in them".

SPEAK LIKE THE GREATS

Take Home Message:

You may not be able to control how others treat you.

You might have every right to get angry.

What you can control, is how you choose to behave.

Never respond or get into an argument with anyone, when angry.

Even if you're right.

Sleep it off.

See how you feel the next day.

Learn to respond without the emotion of anger.

Learn to control your temper.

In doing so, you will become far more proud of the person you are.

Because,

You would have saved, on wounding the hearts of people.

You would have saved, on the regret.

KEVIN ABDULRAHMAN
THE TRIPLE FILTER

One day a man approached Socrates and said, "There's something I need to tell you about your friend".

Wise as he was, Socrates replied, "Before you say anything, let's see if it passes three filters".

"Tell me, do you know this fact to be the truth? Have you checked to make sure it's a fact? That it's undeniably true?", quizzed Socrates.

"No, I don't know that it's true", said the man.

"Interesting. You want to tell me something but you're not sure if it's true or not", remarked Socrates.

"It's what I heard", said the man.

Socrates continued, "Let's test for the the second filter - Goodness.

Tell me, is what you have to say about my friend, good?"

"On the contrary. It's not good at all", said the man.

"You want to tell me something that isn't good about my friend, and yet you don't know if it's absolutely true? Before we jump to conclusions, let's try the third filter - Usefulness.

Is what you have to say about my friend useful to me or anyone for that matter?"

The man shook his head and replied, "Not really".

"If what you have to say isn't true, good or useful, then why bother say it?"

Take Home Message:

Let Socrates' wisdom serve as a reminder to us all.

SPEAK LIKE THE GREATS

THE WORLD IS NOT MADE OF ATOMS. IT'S MADE OF STORIES

Muriel Ruykeser

KEVIN ABDULRAHMAN
TWO SISTERS AND AN ORANGE

Two sisters walk into the kitchen with an objective in mind.

They both want an orange.

Unfortunately for them, there's only one orange in the fruit basket.

And so, like with all loving sisters, a war begins.

"I was here first".

"No I was here first".

"I am the older sister. I get to have it".

"I am the younger sister. I should have it".

This goes on for a few minutes, until in frustration, one sister turns around and tells the other, "Let's just cut the orange in half".

And so they do.

Agreed on a compromise, the orange is sliced in half, and each sister walks away with their half in hand.

A 'win-win' solution.

One sister goes on to juice her half of the orange and throws the skin away.

The others throws the pulp away, and uses the skin to make marmalade.

Not only did they not achieve a win-win.

They both walked away losing.

SPEAK LIKE THE GREATS

Take Home Message:
Both sisters could've had more, had they communicated and worked together.

Had they decided to consider the other person and not just themselves.

They didn't put themselves in the other person's shoes.

They didn't take a moment to ask questions and listen.

They didn't consider the other person's needs.

They could have.

And in doing so, both sisters could have walked away with one whole orange.

The next time you're engaging with your partner, kids, friends, colleague, supplier or customer. Stop, and take a moment to consider what you might be missing?

Ask questions.

Understand their position.

See what's pressing on them.

Get creative.

More often than not, the simple act of putting yourself in other people's shoes, can help you better understand, see and feel their needs.

And in doing so, both you and them can walk away with a whole orange.

KEVIN ABDULRAHMAN
CEO MATERIAL

The CEO of a family business was planning to step down.
Seeking to find the right replacement, he made an announcement to his entire group.
He would search and find his successor from amongst them.

But first, they were all given a challenge.
The winner of this challenge would be the successor.
Each person was given pot, along with a seed.
They all had twelve months to grow their seed in the pot to the best of their ability.
Each person's pot would then be judged.
The winner would become the next CEO.

Like everybody else, one man went home and did what was asked.
As the weeks went by, people at the office spoke about their pots and growing plants.
This man on the other hand, would go home, and regularly care for his pot.
Still, he was unable to see any progress. Nothing was growing in his pot.

Over the coming months, the man grew frustrated.
He would hear everyone at the office speak of how great their plants continued to grow.
And yet, no matter, what he did, his seed didn't grow.
It didn't even break the surface of the soil.
He continued to do everything he could.
He watered it.
Gave it soil fertilizer.
He placed the pot towards the sun.
He would do everything he knew he should.
He was frustrated.
But he persisted.

SPEAK LIKE THE GREATS

Twelve months passed.

It was time for the CEO to judge the pots.

He surveyed the room.

There were great plants everywhere.

Behind each of the pots were individuals who beamed with pride.

Except for one man.

The man who had cared for his seed all year, and still had nothing to show,

Nothing but an empty pot.

The CEO called for the man to step forward.

And then, pointing to him and his bare pot, he announced, "This man is your new CEO".

Chaos ensued.

How could that be?

His pot was empty.

That's when the CEO cut through the chaos and said, "Twelve months ago, I gave you all seeds. I asked you to plant it, water it and take care of it to the best of your ability. But… you were all given boiled seeds. Seeds that couldn't grow.

And yet, apart from this man, somehow you all brought me pots bearing plants.

When your seeds didn't grow.

You replaced it with seeds of your own.

This man was the only person who exhibited courage to continue.

To persist.

To have integrity.

To work on the seed that was given to him.

Despite of it not growing.

Despite of his short term dissatisfaction.

Despite of his frustration of having had to hear about your growing plants.

He is he kind of person I want as my successor.

He is, CEO material.

Take home message:

Remember, it's important that we remain true to our values.

To ourselves. To others. And in what we do.

We should remember that our values aren't for others to see or judge.

Our values are for us.

Our values are to guide us, through life's many temptations.

Because ultimately, in life, we reap, what we sow.

A STORY IS A WAY TO SAY SOMETHING THAT CAN'T BE SAID ANY OTHER WAY

Flannery O'Connor

KEVIN ABDULRAHMAN
A DREAMER

A wise man said, "All the adversity I've had in my life. All my troubles and obstacles, have strengthened me... You may not realize it when it happens, but a kick in the teeth may be the best thing in the world for you."

This man experienced a life filled with challenges, doubts and failures.
Growing up, he was the fourth of five children, in a household that had no money.
As an adult, he struggled to pay rent.
Many evenings, he went without food.
He had creative ideas for characters, but he couldn't even draw.
He was considered, unimaginative.

But this man never let his situation, or his inability, hold him back.
Over time, he created one of the world's most recognizable brands.
He did it without the benefit of a privileged upbringing.
He did it with no handouts.
He did it despite many failures.
He did it after going bankrupt on earlier attempts.

He took out a mortgage on his house to fund his movie, against everyone's advice.
And his most popular character was created at one of the lowest points in his life.

Today, anyone from any generation recognizes this man's name.
His dreams have guided the dreams of children and adults alike ever since.
The dreamer that was Walt Disney.
The man that didn't stop at anything.

The man whose famous creation you know to be Mickey Mouse.
And that movie where he mortgaged his house against - Snow White.

SPEAK LIKE THE GREATS

Take Home Message:

Don't be afraid to dream.

Dream. Then double down and work towards your dreams.

Have no excuse of the situation you're in, or your current inability.

Next time you come up with excuses, think of Walt Disney.

The guy behind Mickey Mouse.

The guy who couldn't even draw.

KEVIN ABDULRAHMAN
WHO'S PACKING YOUR PARACHUTE?

Captain Charles Plumb was a naval jet pilot who had completed 74 combat missions before his plane was shot down.

Ejecting himself out of the plane, he managed to open his parachute, landing safely on the ground.

Captured by the enemy, he was put in prison for 6 years.

Sometime after being released, Charles Plumb was having lunch with his wife at a restaurant.

A man stops and says, "You're Captain Plumb. You flew jet fighters in Vietnam. You were shot down".

To his surprise, Plumb said, "Yes I am. And you're right".

He continues, "How on earth do you know all this?"

The man replies, "I'm the guy who packed your parachute".

Charles Plumb face filled with surprise and gratitude.

The man shakes Plumb's hand and says, "I guess it worked".

Plumb nods, "It sure did. I wouldn't be here if it hadn't".

Plumb didn't sleep that night.

He pondered about how a man whom he did not know held his fate in his hands.

He thought of all the times he would have walked past him without acknowledging him, saying hello, or getting to know him.

After all, Plumb was a pilot. A top gun.

In the limelight. All the action.

This man. He was just a sailor. He packed parachutes at the bottom.

Plumb thought about the hours on end this sailor would have spent packing parachutes. Holding the lives of many in his hands. All whilst going unseen.

SPEAK LIKE THE GREATS

In that moment, Plumb recognized that no one ever plays alone.
That he could have never done all the things he had done, had it not been for the people who supported him.
A team of people, many of them unseen.

Take Home Message:
Realize, a few might be in the limelight, but it's the collective work of a team that brings results.
That save lives.
That give life.
That put a smile on your face.
That facilitate your day.
That ensure you're not going hungry.
That make you feel loved, so you face the day with full force.

There are always many who are behind the scenes.
Who are very often, unseen.

Take a moment to realize and appreciate all the people who directly and indirectly help you do what you do.

Everything we do, we do with, and because of our team.
Only because they go unseen, doesn't mean that they are not important.
Only because they don't desire a medal, doesn't mean they don't deserve recognition.

Who's packing your parachute in life?

KEVIN ABDULRAHMAN
JUST A CROISSANT

Steve Wynn is a known Tycoon.

A billionaire hotelier who has built the Mirage, Treasure Island, the Bellagio, Wynn Las Vegas and Wynn Macau.

One would suspect that a man like him has seen it all.

Yet, when standing up to speak to an audience, he felt there was an 'experience' worth sharing.

Steve drops his wife Elaine and daughter Gillian at the Champs-Élysées Four Seasons Hotel.

In the morning, Gillian orders a croissant.

Rich. Fluffy. Filling.

It's so good, she can only eat half.

The other half she wraps and places in the fridge.

Elaine and Gillian go out for the day.

On their return, Gillian, now hungry, is excited about finishing off the half croissant she'd left.

She goes to the fridge, only to find that the croissant is gone.

"Oh well", she thinks.

"House keeping must have assumed that the half-eaten croissant was left to be thrown away".

They then notice the hotel room phone flashing.

There is a message from house-keeping.

"Thank you for calling", says the house keeper, "We wanted to know when you would arrive so we can send you a fresh croissant. The one you left would have become dry by now."

So impressed was Elaine, that she called her husband Steve to tell him about it.

So impressed was Steve, that he called Issy Sharp, the founder of Four Seasons to tell him about it.

SPEAK LIKE THE GREATS

Why was this so impressive?

What's all the fuss?

All this, for just a croissant?

Well, that's the thing. It wasn't just a croissant.

This wasn't about employee and customer interaction.

This wasn't about service training.

This wasn't about job description.

This was a human being sensing, feeling and acting based on interacting with another human being.

This was a human being putting themselves in the shoes of another, and doing something that anyone would appreciate if it's done for them.

Take Home Message:

It might seem like a simple act.

But it's simple acts like these that are the most profound.

KEVIN ABDULRAHMAN
BREAKING THE UNBREAKABLE

For years and years, the concept of doing a 4-minute mile was deemed dangerous.
Ridiculous.
Unattainable.
Unimaginable.
Impossible.

Runners had tried and failed.
Many had gotten close.
One runner had even managed to get to 4 minutes and 1 second.

But the more runners tried, and failed, the stronger the thought became.
It was man's ridiculous quest to break, an unbreakable barrier.

Roger Bannister, a twenty-five-year old medical student from Oxford University thought he could potentially break the barrier.
He thought that the impossible was possible.
He studied, planned and trained with his team.
On May 6, 1954, after years of people saying that the 4-minute mile was impossible, Roger Bannister, ran the mile.
In 3 minutes. 59 seconds. And 4/10 of a second (3:59.4)

Up until 1954. No one had achieved the impossible.
But soon after this event, it only took 46 days for the barrier to be broken, yet again.

Within three years, close to 20 athletes had broken the 4-minute mile.
Today, over 900 people have broken the 4-minute mile.

SPEAK LIKE THE GREATS

Take Home Message:

What changed?

A thought. A single thought.

Prior to 1954. The thought was, "Can I break it?"

After 1954, the thought became, "How far can I break it by?"

Imagine. The difference.

From just one single thought.

What can a single, powerful thought do for you?

Just imagine, the kind of results you could achieve.

If you started to think that it was possible.

And began making your decisions and taking actions based on that belief.

KEVIN ABDULRAHMAN
TWO BROTHERS

Two brothers worked on a farm.

Every evening, they would go to their respective homes, each with half of what they had harvested for the day.

One of the brothers had a wife and three kids.

The other lived on his own.

They had an agreement. Whatever they made, they shared 50-50.

In the evenings, the single brother would think, "It's not fair that my brother and I are splitting the harvest equally. I'm single. I don't have any dependents. My brother has more mouths to feed. He would be more in need".

So, unbeknown to his brother, every night the single farmer would empty the majority of his harvest and add it to his brother's.

Unbeknown to the single brother, the married one also had a thought. He felt that he was blessed to have a wife and three kids who can take care of him in case something ever happened. On the other hand, his brother was all alone. "What if my brother falls onto difficult times and can't work anymore? Who will take care of him?"

And so, the married brother would also, every evening, take the majority of his harvest and add it to that of his single brother.

Time passed by, and both brothers did this, without knowing what the other was doing.

One evening, they bumped into each other, recognizing why their supply never seemed to have reduced.

They smiled and hugged, realizing that they always had each other's back.

Take Home Message:

Remember. Your care, thought and sacrifice for another is never a loss.

The win is always, far greater.

THERE'S ALWAYS ROOM FOR A STORY THAT CAN TRANSPORT PEOPLE TO ANOTHER PLACE

J.K. Rowling

KEVIN ABDULRAHMAN
WHICH BRICK LAYER ARE YOU?

Three bricklayers were asked, "What are you doing?"

The first bricklayer said, "I'm laying bricks".

The second said, "I'm building a wall".

The third said, "I'm building the House of God".

Take Home Message:

Most people go through their day to day lives like the first brick layer.

Just laying bricks all their life. They are doing a job.

Understand, there is nothing wrong with any job, or having a job.

But it's the limiting mindset, that what you're doing, is just a job.

The difference is evident.

Those with purpose.

Those with a sense of calling.

Those with vision, know.

They know, that they aren't just laying bricks.

These bricks have a purpose.

They have a purpose.

You can see yourself as just having a job.

You can see yourself in a career.

Or you can see yourself, working towards your greater purpose.

No job is meaningless.

It's up to you, to give it meaning.

SPEAK LIKE THE GREATS
LET IT GO

A young boy approached his mother.

His hand inside a vase.

The mother asked him to go place the vase, back where he found it.

He replied, "I can't. It's stuck".

She replied, "Sure you can. You put your hand in. You can get it out".

Again, he said, "I can't mum".

The neck of the vase was narrow.

Somehow the boy had managed to slide his hand in, but now, he was stuck at the wrist.

Growing concerned, the mother called for the father.

The father tried.

No luck.

They tried to use soap, hoping his hand would slide out.

No luck.

In frustration the dad said, "I give up. I'd give ten bucks to figure out how to get his hand out".

As soon as the boy heard this, every one heard a sound of something clinking in the vase, and the boys' hand slipping out.

Surprised, the parents asked, "What happened?"

The boy replied, "I had a penny inside and I was trying to get it out. But when Dad said he would give ten dollars, "I let it go".

Take Home Message:

Often we hold on to what we have, and what we know, unwilling to let go.

We are frustrated, because we are walking around with our hand stuck in a vase.

We can't get rid of it, not because we can't.

But because, we're not wiling to let go.

KEVIN ABDULRAHMAN
HANG THEM UP

A mother faced yet another tough day at work.

For weeks she had been working on a deal, only to find out the competition won the bid.

It was mid-morning when she dropped and broke her phone.

She was due for a promotion, but later in the afternoon, it was announced that no one was receiving bonuses or promotions for the year.

To top it all off, by the end of her day, as she was ready to go home, her car wouldn't start.

The mother called her best friend telling her that it's been a rough day, and asked if she could get a lift home.

As they both approached the front door, the mother went over to a tree that stood outside her home.

Her friend could only make out that she was touching a branch with her finger tips.

And then, as the front door opened, the friend was surprised to see the dramatic change in the mother's face when greeting her children and husband.

As if, none of her day's events had ever occurred.

After dinner, the mother walked her friend to the car.

They passed the same tree, when her friend curiously asked, "What were you doing at the tree when we arrived?"

"Oh, that's my trouble tree", replied the mother.

Seeing the look on her friends' face, she continued, "The tree can't help solve my problems. But the problems I face during the day doesn't belong to my family. I hang them up on the tree before I enter my home. Funnily enough, when I wake up in the morning to pick them up, I find that there aren't anywhere as many problems as what I remember hanging up the evening before".

Take Home Message:

Our days are filled with challenges.

Some more than others.

Many of our worries and concerns are never realized.

Perhaps as you go home today, stop at a nearby tree, and hang your worries on it.

With time, you will notice many of your problems and worries disappear on their own.

And if they don't, this simple act will help you become calmer and more relaxed to finding solutions.

It will also help you better interact with others.

Find a tree, and let it hold on to your worries every night.

KEVIN ABDULRAHMAN
PERFECT IMPERFECTIONS

A water bearer owned two large pots.
They each hung on the end of a stick, which he carried across his neck.
One pot was perfect. It would deliver a full portion of water.
The other was cracked. It only delivered half.

Every day, the water bearer was able to bring back home, the equivalent of one and half portions of water, instead two.

The perfect pot was proud.
The cracked pot, ashamed and disappointed.

One day, the cracked pot spoke to the water bearer.
It told him how it felt like a failure for not being able to give him and his family full portions of water, the way the perfect pot did.

The water bearer said, "Did you notice there were flowers on your side of our daily path?
I've known about your cracks.
That's why I planted seeds on the side of the path.
And you have watered them every day.

I've taken these flowers and placed them in our kitchen table.
It fragrances our home.
It also puts a smile on our family's faces.
Without you being the way you are, we wouldn't have these beautiful flowers to grace our home".

Take Home Message:

Remember, your weakness, could be a strength.

What you see as faults and flaws, could in actual fact be, blessings in disguise.

Your imperfections are perfect.

You just need to change your point of view.

KEVIN ABDULRAHMAN
THAT COMMON FEELING

It was August 2005.

Recently enrolled to university, was a twenty-one-year old named Alex.

Alex was troubled by the thought of coming out of university with a large student loan.

Broke.

Frustrated.

And burdened by what the future held. He thought...

In his room, with a pen and a pad, he brainstormed a few ideas.

"How can I make a million dollars?", he asked himself.

And then. In the simplicity of asking that question, came a crazy idea.

The million-dollar idea.

'The Million Dollar' homepage.

Selling one million pixels on his homepage for a dollar each.

He thought to himself, "This is crazy. But I have nothing to lose".

Armed with only a hundred dollars, and the will to give 'crazy' a try, he bought the domain and set up the site.

Within two days it was live.

Alex struck gold.

In the first month, he sold 250,000 pixels.

That's right, he made two hundred and fifty thousand dollars.

And then, five hundred thousand dollars.

Within four months he had sold the entire space.

All one million pixels sold.

Alex went from being a broke student to a millionaire.

All of it starting from a place of frustration and burden.
Asking the question. Brainstorming.
And willing to give 'crazy' a try.

Take Home Message:
Imagine what you can do.
What ideas do you have?
What ideas can you have if you allow for the 'crazy' to come out freely?

Most people smack their head in disbelief saying, "Why didn't I think of this?"
Often the simplest, craziest ideas that take flight and become success stories are the ones where the person was willing to give 'crazy' a try.

So if you have a crazy idea?
Give it a try.
Your crazy idea, might not be so crazy after all.
Or it might.
No one knows.

Try it.
What have you got to lose?

KEVIN ABDULRAHMAN
ONE MOVE

I heard about a kid that began learning Judo.

He only had one arm. A right arm.

As the weeks went by.

The master taught the kid, a type of a throw.

The kid was ecstatic.

Finally he had learned a move.

In his mind, it was only a matter of time when he would learn more moves.

To his disappointment, that wasn't the case.

His Judo master insisted on him practicing the same throw.

The kid grew in frustration.

All he knew was one throw.

One technique.

All the other kids were learning and doing so much more.

Still. He listened and kept practicing, the same throw.

One day, the kid couldn't take it anymore.

He asked the Sensei, "When will I learn more moves?"

The Sensei replied, "Keep focussing on doing your throw. It's the only move you know. It will be the only move, you will need to know".

Then came the tournament time.

Seasoned and trained Judo players from all over the country arrived.

To everyone's surprise, including the kid's, he won the first two rounds.

The third and fourth were a bit more difficult, but he managed.

He won every fight, and got to the finals.

At the early stages of the finals, it was obvious, the kid was outmatched.

But then, the kid saw an opening, and did his throw.

SPEAK LIKE THE GREATS

His one move.

His only technique.

He pinned his opponent to the ground.

Won the match. And the tournament.

No one was more shocked about the victory than the kid himself.

The kid couldn't help but ask his Sensei how he was able to win?

The Sensei said,

"You won for two reasons.

You didn't just learn a throw. You dedicated all that time and mastered one of the most difficult throws in Judo.

And the only defense for it, is for your opponent to grab your left arm".

Take Home Message:

You might have a disadvantage in life.

Focus, not on your disadvantage.

Focus, on your advantage.

Focus on mastering your advantage.

It will be boring.

It will be frustrating.

Just as it was for the Judo kid.

All you need is to master your throw.

The one throw, that could very will be, the only throw you need to know.

KEVIN ABDULRAHMAN
AND THEN WHAT

Needing a break from his hectic life, a businessman decided to unwind at a coastal village. For a few days, the businessman watched as a fisherman would go out early each day, then come back with a small catch.

One day the businessman decided to get closer to the fisherman.

He complimented the fisherman on his catch and asked, "How long were you out in sea for?"

"Just a few hours", replied the fisherman.

"Have you thought about staying longer and catching more fish?", asked the business man.

"This is more than enough for my family and I", replied the fisherman.

"But you have all this time, what do you do with it?", quizzed the businessman.

"I sleep late. Play with my children. Go for walks with my wife. We have dinner in the village. Meet with friends. Drink. Play the guitar and sing", replied the fisherman.

"What?", the businessman interjected.

"Listen. I can easily help you become more profitable. First of all, you need to spend a few more hours each day at sea. You then sell the extra fish you catch. You save enough to buy another boat. You repeat the process. You do this until you have a fleet of boats".

The businessman then continued,

"You can take this all the way. Cut out the middle man. Get in the markets. Keep an even bigger chunks of the profits.

You can take this across the entire country.

Build a big national business.

Who knows? You can go International. And go really big".

SPEAK LIKE THE GREATS

"How long would all this take?", asked the fisherman.

"About 15 years", replied the businessman.

"And then what?", probed the fisherman.

"At the right time, you can sell your company and make millions", said the businessman.

"And then what?", persisted the fisherman.

"Well, with all the money you have,

You could retire.

You can move to a coastal village.

You can sleep late. Play with your children. Go for walks with your wife. In the evening, you can go for dinner in the village. Meet with friends. Drink. Play the guitar. And sing".

Take Home Message:

Realize - Most people are chasing their tails.

They are chasing their tails because they don't know their truth.

They don't know their truth, because they haven't asked questions.

Questions that would give them clarity about their life.

The kind of life they really wish to have.

Take a moment to ask yourself questions.

And like the fisherman, keep asking yourself, 'And then what?'

Soon enough, that should lead you to your truth.

KEVIN ABDULRAHMAN
IF A FOUR YEAR OLD CAN DO IT

Over a hundred and fifty million dollars raised for cancer research.
And it all started with a four-year-old. Alex Scott.

Alex was born in 1996. Before her first birthday, she was diagnosed with Neuroblastomo, a form of childhood cancer.

In 2000, at the age of four, she told her mother, "When I get out of hospital, I want to have a lemonade stand".

She wanted to give money to doctors, so they could help more kids, like they did her. And she did. Raising over two thousand dollars for her hospital.

Unfortunately Alex passed away in 2004.
But by then, she had inspired many around her to set up lemonade stands.
They had raised over a million dollars.

After Alex's passing, her family continued in honor of her legacy.
Over a hundred and fifty million dollars has been raised by Alex's Lemonade Stand Foundation. Funding 800 research projects at 135 institutions.

All of it, from a four year old's purposeful desire of wanting to help those like herself.

Take Home Message:

What difference do you want to make in the world?
What's your purpose?
What legacy do you want to leave behind?

STORIES CONSTITUTE THE SINGLE MOST POWERFUL WEAPON IN A LEADER'S ARSENAL

Dr. Howard Gardner

KEVIN ABDULRAHMAN
THE BLACK DOT

"We're going to have a quick test", said the professor.
Every student was handed a test-paper, faced down.
The students turned the paper to begin the test.
To their surprise. There were no questions.
Just a black dot.

The professor asked the students to answer the question - "What do you see?"
Every student began writing their thoughts.

Once done, the professor then gathered their papers.
He began reading through their answers.

Everyone had written about the black dot.
It's position.
It's context.
It's significance.
The black dot was the focus.

The professor then exclaimed, "It's interesting how none of you wrote about the rest of the page. All the white space".

Take Home Message:

Your life has plenty of white space in it.

Yet often, you'll find yourself only focussing on the black dot.

The restraints of resources.

Your temporary issues.

Problems, and challenges.

You focus on the black dot, and miss the entire white space.

You focus on the black dot, and miss on all the beauty in life.

Realize and remember.

There is more to your life than the black dot.

KEVIN ABDULRAHMAN
SAME MARKET, DIFFERENT RESULTS

Two sales reps, from two different shoe companies travel to Africa.

They are to establish whether there are opportunities to expand into a new market.

Within a few days, the two sales people get on the phone, each speaking to their respective leadership team.

The first salesperson says, "I have been looking around and frankly speaking, I don't see any opportunities here. I think we should stick to where we are. Let's not waste our money on this market'.

The CEO questions, "Well, why not?"

The salesperson utters (with a long sigh for dramatic effect) in absolute disappointment, "It's pointless. No one here wears shoes".

Now, the other salesperson makes a similar call to update his team.

He says, "Prepare the manufacturing plant to increase production. I need you to make things happen and have a container packed with shoes sent to me, right away".

Hearing the enthusiasm and excitement in the salesperson's voice, the CEO can't help but ask, "What's with the excitement? What makes you think there's even a market for these shoes? We've even heard the competitor has looked at this market and decided not to go ahead".

Bursting at the seam with energy, the salesperson turns around and says, "You have no idea how beautiful this market is. It is absolutely untouched.

No one here is wearing shoes.

With a bit research, a lot of hard work and persistence, this entire market can be ours for the taking.

We will have first movers advantage and dominate the marketplace".

Take Home Message:

Same industry.

Same environment.

Same market.

Two different individuals.

Two different results both for themselves, and ultimately the outcome for their companies.

Opportunities are everywhere.

One sees no opportunities.

The other, only sees opportunities.

Your results today is a reflection.

A reflection of beliefs, thoughts, decisions and actions.

Of yourself. And that, of your people.

Realize - The quality of your results is a direct reflection of the quality of your mind.

KEVIN ABDULRAHMAN
WHAT CAN YOU DO?

Mark is awesome.

He works at a salon where the starting price for a haircut is $150.

His clients? Celebrities.

His only day off is Sunday.

You might think that this is a day of relaxation.

Well, not for Mark.

He goes out to New York City giving free haircuts to the homeless.

On the streets. Sidewalks. Park benches. On top of crates.

Sunshine or rain. Mark gets on with it.

He believes that a haircut or beard trim can transform a person's demeanor.

He also believes that everyone should feel good about themselves.

And so if they can't afford to have a haircut or beard trim, Mark will give it to them.

Take Home Message:

Giving isn't about having a million dollars to give.

Giving isn't about having all the resources in the world.

Giving isn't about showing others how much you are doing.

Giving is about doing what you can.

With what you have. In your very own way.

To be like Mark. To maybe, help others feel good about themselves.

In every one of us, there is something that we can give.

To help lift another human being.

The world needs more people with the heart and soul of Mark.

The world needs more people like you.

SPEAK LIKE THE GREATS
THE SEVEN WONDERS OF THE WORLD

Kids in a class were asked to write down the seven wonders of the world.
Though some struggled, many of them, after looking over each other's shoulders were able to write some of them down.

When the teacher quizzed the kids - they began mentioning wonders like,

The Great Wall of China
The Taj Mahal in India
The Grand Canyon in the U.S
The Pyramids Of Egypt
Hagia Sophia in Turkey
Machu Picchu in Peru
Victoria Falls in Zimbabwe

One kid wasn't contributing.
She seemed deep in her thoughts, unfazed by what the other kids were saying.
The teacher asked if she had something to add?
She nodded and said, "I'm not sure if I have all the wonders, but I think the real seven wonders of the world are, our ability

To See. To Touch. To Taste. To Hear. To Feel. To Laugh. And To Love.

Take Home Message:
We search the world for wonders. And we overlook the simplest things.
The many things we have been blessed with, that we take for granted.
And although there are indeed many great wonders in our world.
The greatest of wonders, reside right within every single one of us.

KEVIN ABDULRAHMAN
SNAP THAT TOOTHPICK

A man goes to the circus.

As he gets to the entrance, he walks past a few elephants.

To his surprise, they're not locked in giant cages. They aren't even held by thick chains.

Instead, they're held by a tiny piece of rope that's pegged to the ground.

Curious, the man stops to ask the trainer how an elephant can be held by a tiny rope.

These magnificent and massive creatures could easily flick the rope and snap the peg, just as easily as you and I would snap a toothpick.

The trainer replies, "When the elephants are much smaller, the tiny rope is enough to hold them down. They try, and try, and try. But over time realize that they just can't get away.

Now that the elephants have grown up, they still hold the belief, that they can't break free".

Take Home Message:

What past beliefs are you holding onto?

So what if you couldn't do it in the past?

So what if you tried and failed?

So what if you weren't good enough?

Your past does not dictate your capabilities today.

Your past does not dictate your future.

The only thing holding you back today, is you.

You're not a baby elephant. Stop acting like one.

Snap that mental tooth pick pegging you down.

Get up. Go.

STORYTELLING IS THE MOST POWERFUL WAY TO PUT IDEAS INTO THE WORLD

Robert McKee

KEVIN ABDULRAHMAN
HAPPINESS IS WHAT YOU HAVE

There was crow who lived in the forest.
Life was good.
Until the day he saw a beautiful swan.
He thought to himself, "She's so beautiful. She's so white. And I'm so black. She must be the happiest bird in the world."

To confirm his theory, he asked the swan if she felt like the happiest bird?
"Actually," the swan replied, "I was feeling like I was the happiest bird around. Until I saw the parrot. I'm white. But he has two colors. I now believe that the parrot is the happiest bird."

The crow then approached the parrot to confirm whether he was the happiest.
The parrot responded by saying, "My life was great. I thought I was happy. Until I saw the magnificent multicolored feathers of the peacock. That peacock is bound to be the happiest bird".

The crow then went to the zoo to meet with the peacock.
Hundreds of people were taking pictures of the peacock all day.
The crow waited until everyone had left before he asked, "Tell me peacock, are you the happiest bird of us all? You must be. Look how beautiful you are."

The peacock replied, " I always thought I was beautiful, until I realized that my beauty was the reason I'm trapped in the zoo. Come to think of it, of all the birds that I have seen, the crow is the only bird that is never caged. Recently I've been thinking, that if I was a crow, I would be free. And I would be the happiest bird in the world."

Take Home Message:

Stop comparing yourself with others.

You never know what their lives are like.

Accept what you have.

Embrace who you are.

Realize that you're made the way you are, because you serve a greater purpose.

Believe that.

You already have happiness.

You just need to realize it.

KEVIN ABDULRAHMAN
IT'S DAMAGED

A man went on site to visit a sculptor.

As he glanced around, he noticed a statue.

It was crafted with such accuracy.

And so he marveled at the great piece.

Just as he was about to compliment the sculptor on his work, the man's eye caught another statue.

On closer look, he realized, it was exactly the same statue.

Puzzled, the man asked, "Why do you have two of the same statue?"

The sculptor replied, "The first one was close to completion, when it got damaged".

The man looked at the 'supposedly damaged' one for a bit.

He couldn't find anything wrong with it.

The sculptor then pointed to the nose, "There is a scratch on his nose. My chisel accidentally slipped".

The man said, "You can't even see that. No one would ever know it was there".

The sculptor replied, "But I would".

SPEAK LIKE THE GREATS

Take Home Message:

There will be many times in life where you can easily slip things under the rug.

Things that many will never notice.

Things that no one will never know even exist.

But you, will always know.

Excellence isn't something that's done for the sake of others.

It's done for the satisfaction of your own heart.

It's a representation of who you want to be.

It's the symbol of everything you stand for.

It's the legacy you will be known for.

KEVIN ABDULRAHMAN
I FEEL FOR YOU

I heard about an iPad 2 that was returned to Apple soon after it was launched.

The VPs kept a close eye on their returns to check for faults and any issues that required immediate attention.

This return stood out, for a totally different reason.

One that they hadn't encountered before.

In all his excitement, a man had purchased the iPad 2, without the counsel of his wife.

Needless to say, the message was made clear to him - It had to be returned.

And so, with his tail between his legs, he returned it, with a sticky note that read,

"Wife said NO"

The executives at Apple got wind of the story.

They decided to send it back to him.

A few days later, the customer received his iPad 2, with a different note that read,

"Apple said YES"

Take Home Message:

Empowered employees have the ability to empathize.

And do something about it.

When you create a culture where your people feel empowered.

They can place themselves in the shoes of their customer.

They can feel and sense what they are feeling.

And in turn, they can think of simple, creative ways, to build the kind of goodwill that will turn customers into raving fans.

SOMETIMES REALITY IS TOO COMPLEX. STORIES GIVE IT FORM

Jean Luc Godard

KEVIN ABDULRAHMAN
MAKE THE PROMISE

It was 1968. The summer Olympics was being held in Mexico city.

A young man from Tanzania created an impression, one that would last far beyond that day.

His name? John Stephen Akhwari.

John took part in the marathon.

A race that is a true test of one's mental and physical strength.

74 people started that race.

Only 57, finished it.

I wish I could tell you that John came first.

He didn't.

I wish I could tell you that John came in the top three.

He didn't.

John didn't even come last - or so the officials had thought.

He came in over an hour and a half later, after what the judges had initially thought was the last person to cross the finish line.

The winners' ceremony had been completed.

The medals were handed to the respective winners.

Spectators were leaving the stadium… When suddenly, they were informed about a man hobbling towards the stadium.

Early on the race, John fell and hurt his knee.

In actual fact, he had dislocated his knee - A notable challenge considering a working knee joint is imperative when competing in a marathon.

Bandaged and bloody, John still got up, and continued with his quest of moving forward.

SPEAK LIKE THE GREATS

John was slow.
But he kept on going.
John was in excruciating pain.
But he kept on going.

He hobbled into that stadium.
Finally crossing the finish line.

When John was asked why he kept going despite the pain?
He replied,

**"My country did not send me 5000 miles to Mexico City, to start the race.
My country sent me 5000 miles, to finish the race".**

Take Home Message:
Friends, I want you to know.
Your race will be full of challenges and obstacles.
Your race will be filled with falls.
Your race will have you broken, bloody and bandaged.

But it is on you, to keep going.
It's on you to make the promise.

The promise, to never quit.
The promise, to do what ever it takes.
The promise, to finish, your race.

KEVIN ABDULRAHMAN
FINAL WORDS

Please read and re-read the short stories.

Practice them. By speaking them out loud.

Anywhere. Everywhere.

Recognize the pattern of how the stories are set up.

The audience must get and <u>feel</u> your message - without any further explanation.

Practice delivering them, and as you do, you will be able to mold it to your style.

Accept every opportunity you get to speak.

The more you practice, the more natural it becomes.

The more confident you become.

The more fun you will have.

That's how 'The Greats' do it.

Welcome to the club.

Your friend,

Kevin Abdulrahman

SPEAK LIKE THE GREATS
LEADERS TAKE NOTE

You are the face.
You are the brand.
You are the leader.

There is an expectation of you to speak with impact. From everyone.
I mean, everyone.

You need to deliver on that expectation.
There is no faking it.
There is no escaping it.

Get coached.
Leadership communication is critical to your credibility and competence.

If you're a CEO, world leader or president who requires confidential, results-driven advisory, my office can be reached on

info@KevinAbdulrahman.org

YOU DON'T HAVE TO BE GREAT TO START. BUT YOU HAVE TO START, TO BE GREAT

Zig Ziglar

www.ingramcontent.com/pod-product-compliance
Lightning Source LLC
Chambersburg PA
CBHW051327220526
45468CB00004B/1526